Fifty Poems
Five Decades
Fifty Thousand Miles

David W. Erskine

outskirts
press

Dedication

This book is dedicated to my daughters Chloe and Noelle. It is also dedicated to Elizabeth, their wonderful mom and although we are not together, have maintained a great friendship. A special shout out to Erik, Chloe's partner, and Hot Buttered Rum (his incredible band) and Taryn, Noelle's partner, with a heart and smile as big as a towering redwood tree. Also, my friend and mentor Tinoa Rodgers. It is also dedicated to my parents John, and Inge along with my siblings Erika, Bebo (Liz), John, Kathy, and Peter. Also, to Erika's late husband Max, their children Sue, her husband Peter, Max, his wife Heike, and John as well as their grandchildren Hunter, Rebeckah, Cedric, and Cecilia. Thank you to my sister Liz's husband Chuck and children Linda, Janet, Karen, Roger, Barbara, and Alison Prine. Thank you to John's wife Cindy, and children Sharon, Chris, and Kate. Thank you, Peter's wife Laura, and children Sean and Elena. My German family includes Aunt Erika, Uncle Pitt, cousin Sabine, Uncle Hermann, Aunt Erika, and children Ursula, Barbel and her daughter Julia. Dedicated to Rainer the Burger Meister of Finikounda, his wife Petra, and children Camilla and Marek aka Drummer and Squire. Special thanks to my Godson Nick Tsairides, my producer, his brother Mike and parents Demos and Cathy. Also, to the entire Cardillicchio family Rosie, David, Gabriel, Carol, Kayla, Nikki, Lauren, Maureen, Chris, Sarah, Blake, Nick, and Melissa. Finally, I would never and cannot forget Domingo and Buckles!

Contents

Introduction

This book of poetry began in the summer of 1971 on Lake Traunsee in Gmunden, Austria. It contains fifty poems over five decades and fifty thousand miles. It is meant to provide joy, discovery, and an opportunity to share my journey. It is dedicated to my daughters Chloe and Noelle, who have always been great travelers. The poems were a way for me to capture my journey but also a way to process that journey over five decades.

It is also dedicated to my parents, John Ardis Erskine and Inge Leske Erskine, who raised six children and always inspired us to travel worldwide throughout our lives. I am grateful that they had the vision to support our journeys wherever they took us.

There are five chapters. The 70s were written while traveling in Western and Eastern Europe, on to Greece and Turkey before finally driving overland to India and back. The 80s include being a taxi driver and actor in Boston and LA. The 90s include the birth of my daughters in LA and moving to San Francisco. The 2000s include a sales career in startups and tech companies as well as return trips with my daughters and our German family to Italy, Paris, and Leipzig. The 2010s opened with a new career in sales coaching and consulting, the bliss and beaches of Kailua, a return to writing poetry, blogging, and discovering the joy of Stoicism.

1970s Decade of Poems

Acting Class

Brown ceiling glances
upon actors/actresses.
His bedazzled eyes/expression
push hands toward
defensive shock.
Adjacent encounter has
him glancing elsewhere
overshadowed by women.
Bags of nails drop
to floors below
actresses/actors.
Their expressions frozen
clockwise yet forevermore
entertaining/enlightening.

January 1973

Friendship

Suddenly things fall together
worn ink-stained hands
feel excitement life again.
Existence is worth all ounces.
Friends fumble forward
in unison.
Alone yet always accompanied.
My friends are my life
happiness strength,
all coasting back.

February 1973

Breeze

Leaving my feet
hang from a window.
Sliding out upon
glass riddled pavement.
Breezes blow across
My breast.
Air cools my thighs.
Present position
posits new thoughts.
Rain wrinkles shoes.
Delicious sweat orders
another oder.

St. Patrick's Day

Wind settles through.
Hearty burgundy
decides to bring
another day along with it.
Determining its own free form
much like these lines,
structured perhaps
temperature-wise
massively inundated.
into tornados,
while uniquely separated
listening to itself timely
from crooks/crevices.

Political Musings

Descended as rain.

The asphalt is sharp.

What's to be done.

about the revolution?

Infatuations drawn easily.

simply.

The trees' weather themselves

seasonally.

Quiet clocks lose sense of time.

I lose my sense of rhyme.

Ancient posters repress

desperation.

A desperation which can't

be repressed anymore.

Clothing Speaks

Humor ridden
saddled with smiles.
Today thin breezes
mask me,
Placate humidity.
Worn out sneakers laugh
occasionally, though their holes
colors unravel from dissolved soles.
Snickering shirts smirk
sarcastically
dancing in delight.
We all enjoy this
general state
of confusion.

Simply Summer

Summer struggles forward

Leaves laugh

trees tumble

Nature provides comfort.

Companions appear.

friendships grow

warmth dallies about

problems disappear

Momentarily.

Life regains simplicity

we untangle ourselves

trying to help.

Happiness flounders by

wrapping around us

comforting

relaxing

our souls.

Our bodies dangle/dance

simultaneously.

Baudelaire

Sunday morning,
wandering t-shirt,
Ear scratched cat
We call Bo.
She stretches out
waiting.
Strange women solemnly
stroll on by,
almost melancholy, seemingly subdued,
occasionally oppressed.
Spreading a short beard
through and about Bo's head
she remains in the bed.
women have passed, Bo commands
her window view.

Baudelaire the Cat

Bo comes alertly
selecting all steps
carefully/cautiously
protecting life
under her belly
not indulging pain
Perhaps surrounded by it.
Leaving pains possibility
to each encounters eye
lying about ripe
rich exhausted.

Baudelaire It's a Wrap

No animosity
inside me.
Competitiveness
lacking.
Another Sunday
morning sleeping late,
lying about
writing becomes habitual.
Empty room
clothes provide color
Bo provides affectionate.
glances.
Her closing eyes
perpetual pose
sensitive ears
are embraced.

1980s Decade of Poems

Friendship

Friendship to me

is acceptance, openness

willingness to let me be me

relax breath live the moment.

Others can accept me for me.

Let me be the dad I am.

Trust in me

that optimism will prevail.

If you cannot do it.

Friendship slips away

for me.

Cambridge Winter Day

Wind knocked out of me
today.
Sunken Posture
contorted stomach
Recoiling.
Clarity pervades every
thought.
Love emerges.
Strength recoils
as I start anew
it's easy
a similar dynamic
only in another direction.
Life continues to draw
amazing new forms,
as the sun's golden leaves
dot an icy windowpane.

Wind Chilled February

This clenched fist
Rapped in bloodied towel.
Swollen over.
Frustration ably applies
kindly douche our minds
Re- enter naked thoughts
taking it from the top.
Wind chills spines
bringing me down
rubbing ego
erases itself.
Light scene turns dark
electric brain cells
coordinating a change
collective illumination.

Grace

Hello my dear,

what grace you

drop my way.

Tenderness on spring eves

you collect for me.

Understanding of knowledge

intertwined with depth/Caring.

Examples float like

trial balloons.

Filled with joy from your breath.

Oh, how much has been dropped

near my soul,

Without barely asking.

What grace you

drop my way.

Lucky Man

Dream dissolves
to sunshine / spring
Dabbling delicately
With life's treasures.
It's fragile
as trembling fawns.
One feels pawn-like
In a well-armed world.
Yet dreams pass
through, bringing
us closer to ourselves.
Acting stints
blossomed tenderness
new- born friends
life cycling about.
Never forget
I'm a lucky man.

Stuck in the Muck

He was undecided to the end

sidetracking shuffling along

alone.

Bearing his heart only

to his mind,

Mindless of community

re-enforced delusions.

Proof offers nothing but oneself,

recycles articles of livid hood or level head.

Requiring more backpedaling

less movement.

Summer Breeze

Thursday descending
half-moon ushers it in
scattered lights begin
existence acknowledged.
Unsettled stomach
accompany me.
Fences abound incapable,
of maintaining Thursday.
Accelerating now
not glancing back
becoming sole possessor
of following events
descending Thursday.

Midnight

Midnight
let's tangle stars together.
Light reflecting one thousand
directions.
Etching our minds
delicately until
we discover one another.
Tracing our touch.
Outlining all features
continuing a character
realizing it is us.
Together smiling
no glowing yes beaming
purple hugs melt
my gray-blue colors
to ecstasy.

Infinity

Relaxed eyes
hallucinate upon doors.
Perhaps anticipating another
time/place.
Perhaps wishing another
time/place.
However still focusing
on the same.
My eyes fade toward
infinity, clocked by time
illustrating its own uselessness.
I will fade with today
into tomorrow.

1990 Decade of Poems

Purple Haze

Back to the beginning

Move away from the haze

Return to the 3rd floor in Jamaica Plain

The lonely walks until Spring found me

The new seeds of life in all of us.

While sifting through the Santa Ana Winds

That haunt the Southland

Uneventful weekend of car searching.

Don't look for the joy

Find the joy.

Glow with it. Don't surrender

Break out of it.

Why? Because otherwise you are the

Plain haze

Disappearing into the dust

Not challenging but remaining the same.

Over and over again

Take the different course, if suits you

To a tee. Now laugh with glee.

Daughters Smiles

To my girls with your smiles

Our smiles are rings that hold

Our hands together.

You make me a better dad, person friend

With your smiles.

I will keep learning as you teach me

How to smile

Again, and again

And again.

Your open hearts fill our house

With love, life smiles.

We will walk many millions of miles

Because of your smiles

Create a road

Filled with joy

Filled with change

Filled with love.

I am the luckiest dad in the world

Because of you

My girls

And your smiles.

New Decade

Reflection on a decade gone by

No time to wail or sigh

Just an early goodbye

Look toward your next step

Climb to your lovers' arms

_____ her tears to some distant form

Let your child grow.

The future looks bold

The new decade will help dissolve

Past weakness insecurities & fears

Believe me buddy you & the bride

Have many years to explore

The wonder of California

Life itself.

Relax you are going to be complete.

Los Angeles

Moving forward to a new coast

Completed the journey and found

The breath of freshness

Cannot control my fingertips

We found new love in

Collective past.

We are children

Like we were then.

The cycles return to give us the

New glimpse

The train departed from South Station

Only to find L.A. along the way

Thank you for sharing the West Coast

With us today.

Trust

To talk of trust

Let us bid ourselves to be human.

Look inward before outward

Dwell into personal depths

To find peace of mind.

All know life is kind

When it is left alone.

Mistrust dissolves life into

Meaningless mirages

Untrample yourself,

See your own joy

Its importance shall radiate

All things everywhere.

Solitude

Family at work

I anxiously await their return

Clean house, paid bills, chores done

Yet loneliness is palpable

In the air so to speak.

TV off Tony Bennett on

I welcome Snoopy's dinner time.

More reflections on a solitary day.

It has been so very long

But it is not missed.

Remember those who

Do not want to be alone.

I know understand comprehend them

It can feel like the setting sun.

Rock Gardens

Time to restructure.

That rock garden

Into its timeless forms.

Letting plants

Flower their way

To freedom.

We all try to get there.

Momentary delays

Increase rocky efforts

Yet solidify our resolve.

Tenderizing forms,

Rocks concealed within

Our grasp

Finally leading us

To new heights

These rock gardens

Are always shifting

Similar to their planters.

They refuse to be placed

Only in one spot

Never to move

Because they always will.

Pinecones

Dropping their wares
Into sheltered needles.
Finding a way
To weather themselves
For tomorrow trees.
Creating new homes
From singular loneliness.
Circles of happiness
Adorn our homes
Giving pause
To local customs
And holidays
Simplicity of cyclical notions
Gives us nature
And nature
And nature us,
Both smiling
At our united front
Of tenderness.

Loneliness

Loneliness drips down my cheek

Looking for Mama

To talk, laugh, share

Yet I know she is there.

Constant confusion

East west direction

Must be time to ride the bike stationary

To get remain health.

Remember better days are now not then not tomorrow

Early to say hard to live by

Seeking quality all around, yet loneliness surrounds

Am I an oddball on a separate planet?

Reflections on much gone by, vacations

Family dynamic

Holding me together like glue.

Time to smile at Mama hold her near

Know that she lives all around me

The confusion is a guide

Do not be afraid or hide.

Driving

Soaked in mist

Hair hangs briefly

Taken for a ride

Shaken in a walk

Found sand beneath me

Gentle ocean seas.

Found you driving

Steering a new course.

We, passing together again

Joys of driving

At similar speeds

Not stalling

Simply calling

I am relaxed again.

2000 Decade of Poems

Distance

The circular return to who

We really be.

Not that far from me.

Blue sky is the key

To Mama/me.

We experience life together

Yet-you-bet

We learn to be one family

Like the tree

You/me/family

Though distance can seem far

It's only a spec on my sleeve

Now how far can that be.

Mama

Grey Maroon Sky

Will not dampen our spirits.

Trip to touch Mama's relatives' home

Places of delight

Will etch our adventure into ourselves

For many moons ahead.

We learned the language all over again

We shared European history, tradition & people

With the ones that live here

We brought Chloe to understand

Her grandmother for future travels.

We reconnected our love.

To tighten our family ties.

We each one of us touched Mama

By being here.

Chloe

Beautiful Chloe taking the snooze

Gently pacifying herself.

Creating love life

To her mom/dad.

Knowing her growth continues

To happen now that

One week birthday has arrived.

We learn yet once more

That Chloe is what it's about.

Loving, engaging here and everywhere

Thank you, my daughter,

For giving much to mom and dad

The very thing we never had

You.

Noelle

With both my wonderful girls

taking a snooze

Life can feel just right

The ease of their sleep

Can relax me too.

The joy of life with the family here

Make me display one big smile

We can be lucky to the tee

Thank my girls for making life

The way we like it to be.

Thank you for your yawns

Your sleepy gaze

Your very lovely ways.

Keep the dreams in your look

No time to read the book

Thank you, my girls, for being here.

Stinson Beach

Redwoods embrace the dusk

As the road

Melts toward the Pacific.

Lone deer spot a familiar climb

Glancing back on the disappearing dusk

Spotting headlights in the sky.

Beyond light banter

Enjoyable conversation collapses

Toward yesterday's dreams.

Comfortable distances return

Leaving today blanketed

By preconceived foes.

Homemade spaghettis hope

Waits yet again

Drifting far away.

Horizon

Dreams traveling here

Lifting me beyond

Sitting with change

Watching fires glow

Beautiful talented love

Rewarding the gentle ones.

Friendship floats effectively

New moments linger

I leap beyond

Low tides.

Floating over rocks

Presence compelled remaining

Nearby me.

To my dear love

To know

My time's coming.

Shooting Star

When the moon rises to sleet

Those who give

It will sparkle past those

Who don't,

And never did.

Self-involvement turns

One inward

Like the sea

Turning brown

Leaving the thoughtless

Spinning inward with

Limited growth.

Remember my friend

To stand tall

Shoulders back

Moving like the shooting star

Continually, through beyond within

Creating galaxy of timeless time

Sunshine

Let the sunshine inward

Give yourself credit

For all the little things you do.

Great dads don't just arrive

The process is ongoing taking years

Tears and Fears

It all adds up.

From L.A. to the Summit

Now the Manor

Open up to the possibilities

Not the limitations.

Release the what ifs

Let the sunshine in

It will be okay

Because you are there

Just don't know it yet.

Lake Superior

Begin with breathing

Leave judging at the door

Say no more.

Observe with Lake Superior

Journey anew with the girls

Time to test new waters.

All together now

Breeze across our faces

Combining us down different avenues.

We walk our own way

Yet blend as one family

With new power

Words are there

But not heard

Occasionally hugs appear.

Building fires

Keep our hearts

A glow with love.

Foundation is solid

Place to feel rooted

Like a multi-colored quilt

Our smiles gently

Tilt toward each other

Laughter captures each moment

We know how

Powerful our ties

Keep us whole.

It brings our hands atop

One another

As the sun glows with love so great.

Sit and Stew

Back to the beginning

Missing my girls

What to do

Sit and stew.

Pain is here

Doesn't seem to want

To disappear

Keep the moment?

Back to the beginning

Where the blue sky

Stretches between

Our windows

We touch magically

Our voices meet

Down the distant street.

Will the writing take hold

Mold a new feeling?

Sit and Stew Part 2

Wandering back

To distant feelings

Of loneliness.

Back to the beginning

It must be the place.

My heart is given to my girls

Only normal the emptiness

It holds when

The distant street

Seems so far.

Back to the beginning

To find myself

Connected with the moment.

Back to the beginning

Where pop-fly's are caught

Lines are read and hugs are given.

Back to the beginning

Where we'll grow

Closer by the distance

That bind us

Together as one family

2010 Decade of Poems

Madrid

Middle Plateau

Newly found city

Captures sun wind history

Together.

Cousin from the East

collects a sibling and a son

To join the adventure

Super Bowl soccer Grand Evening Game

In the plaza

Expresso and chocolate desserts

Embrace.

The Three Musketeers

Amid laughter, hugs, and joy

Graceful Madrid is touching

Each of our hearts

Multiple times today

Yesterday and tomorrow.

Iberia Collection of Moments

Firm release

It is very liberating

In a long awaited

Liberated country.

Does this entitle anyone?

No, there comes that form

Once again.

Stay honest to the feelings

Of love and endless giving.

It is not the ability

To spend, it is the

Formless attachment

To it.

Girls gave to me this week

In cooking, talking, hugging

Sharing books, quiet walks

In the park or being on their own.

Kailua

Lone loons linger

Silent sunglasses sit

Water woes weaves

Ankle arms artfully

Toward tinder toe

Healthy holding happens

For find friends

Sun sits somewhere

July in Kailua joyfully

Ears elbow East

Towards those thoughts

Charming caring Chloe.

West to East

A bit melancholy

As Chloe departs

We are close

In many ways

Very finely tuned

And attached together

The evolving continues

Across the continent

We teach one another

We laugh fully

We do so completely

And show it continually.

Mahalo

Island breezes flow

Through me and beyond

Darling evening sun

Sparkles and shimmer

All around

Waves share

Their sounds

Of silence

Over a July sunset

Gratitude

Saturday night blues

Alone again

The Pacific below

sending kind waves

Toward my soul

Filling the void

With wonderous love

Grateful gratitude now

Embracing every pore

Rippling gentle reminders

Of old days

Grateful for what I have

Do not worry about

What you think you need.

Let Us Begin

Looks like I am walking

Eyes wide open

Amid new adventure

Including gentle solitude

Perhaps some loneliness

Being direct and honest

With my needs

as these support

Kindness to others

Turning to forgiveness

Of myself completely

Being not afraid.

Letting the flow

Of daily life

Inspire new creativity

Building better ties

A healthier world

Gravity of spirit

Fog Laden Clouds

Fos laden clouds

Below blue sky

White, blue green

Color my way to a new day

It is all new

Like a landscape

Of visual images

Beckoning to me

Please do not ignore

This present moment

Fog laden clouds

Say "Thank You"

To the blue

Say "Lovely Scene"

To the green

Say "Embrace the Day"

To the Fog laden way.

Autodesk

Departing the "Desk"

Brings real reflection

How to communicate?

The next chapter

Is it necessary?

Who it helps

Me them they?

Cold calms me

Slows me down

Assists in cramming

Today and tomorrow

Get to health

Let others give

The needed friendship

Let them go

celebrate your solitude

Embrace it fully

Let it flow all through you.

Pre-Dawn Blues

Pre-dawn blues

After oh so many years

Here amid mountains

Yet ocean nearby

Under dark blue sky

Pre-dawn blues

Time to change

Whether to want

For gentle touch

Patience is poked

Ego needs stroked?

Pre-dawn blues

Brings back decades

Of written lines

Many embracing each other

Thoughts return

Opens my mind

To those pre dawn blues.

www.ingramcontent.com/pod-product-compliance
Lightning Source LLC
LaVergne TN
LVHW090722290325
807212LV00007B/168